PRAISE

C000225469

'As well as being a very successful care provider, whose attention to detail is second to none, Kemi has written a book that comes just at the right time to de-mystify the entire CQC registration process and provide much-needed guidance to prospective care providers wishing to go/going through CQC registration. It provides information in an easy-to-understand and follow format to support qualified candidates on their journey to becoming registered care providers in England. I encourage you to go through this book alongside the guidance provided by the CQC to make the entire process as stress-free as possible and increase your chances of being registered with the CQC.'

Nya Mabu Ngwashi
Owner of Connect Care Consultancy and coach

'An indispensible guide to navigating the many considerations in becoming a good/outstanding care provider.'

Nana Banton
Abacus Care & Support

'This book is full of useful and essential information that deals with the minefield of CQC registration. It covers all the different aspects that are needed to start a business in the sector and for anyone contemplating a business in the care sector, this book will be indispensable. Recognising that there has never been a better time to start a business in care, this book will help anyone who is considering working to provide care, to start strongly and pave their way to success.'

Abimbola Ladipo-Aridegbe
Parent and Child Fostering Services

GETTING INTO CARE

HOW TO BUILD A SUCCESSFUL DOMICILIARY AND SUPPORTED LIVING BUSINESS

KEMI MADUMERE

First published in 2022 by

Panoma Press Ltd

www.rethinkpress.com

www.panomapress.com

Cover design and book layout by Neil Coe

978-1-784529-73-4

I would like to dedicate this book to my biggest supporters, my amazing husband, Chris, and daughter, Ashlynn, who have always been my biggest fans, and to the people who inspire me to do better to serve them each day.

Contents

Introduction

You are choosing a good time to to start a business in care: demand for all kinds of care is high and is only likely to increase. If you are considering setting up a business in this sector, this book will get you started on your journey and provide you with the tools and resources you need to succeed. It will support you to navigate the processes and requirements of Care Quality Commission (CQC) registration and covers everything else that is needed to start a business in the care sector.

The information provided in this book draws on my knowledge of and experience in the industry, gathered over the course of setting up my care company and property management firm. This book also features expertise from industry specialists, both from the care sector and, to some extent, the property industry, who have agreed to share their insights, knowledge and business skills with you.

My story

I come from a family of business owners and, over the years, my love of running businesses has developed. I have enjoyed periods of great success and, equally, times where things didn't go so well. In each circumstance, I took everything, the good and the bad, as an opportunity to learn, grow and identify areas for improvement.

I launched my first business when I was just eleven, setting up a local kids' club, followed by a string of businesses funded by various organisations including the Prince's Trust. Up until a few years ago, over a period of seven years, Chris (my husband) and I successfully ran a property company specialising in providing flatshares for young professionals in central London. The business was based on a rent-to-rent model, where we leased properties long term from landlords and re-let them to university students and interns who were new to the UK. When the UK decided to leave the EU and several property and tax laws were changed, our business, like many others, suffered a serious downturn. We recovered, but not to the level at which we had previously been operating. Of course, this was then further impacted by the coronavirus pandemic. We did learn a valuable lesson, however: never put all your eggs in one basket.

In 2018 we were attending a property seminar that covered a small segment of the care industry, specifically supported living premises or transforming properties into such. I felt it was a niche area of the property world but it struck a chord with us. Sourcing and providing supported living homes felt similar to the business we were already running, except in this case we would be providing support as well as housing for vulnerable adults.

We obtained our CQC licence registration swiftly. The challenging part was getting clients on board, especially from the local authority – and during a pandemic.

2

Like most new providers, we had no CQC rating yet and so were regarded as inexperienced. Nevertheless, we persisted and successfully negotiated contracts and secured local authority clients within twelve months of our registration. Our care business has since grown from strength to strength and we have ambitious plans for it.

With some business acumen, passion for what you do and a deep understanding of your target clientele, there is no reason you can't achieve the same level of success, and more. I want to help you build a thriving business of which you are proud. In this book, I will walk you through the different stages of establishing and registering a CQC-qualified business, step by step, explaining the entire process from the initial application through to getting your first clients. I share the key actions and assets that have led to our success: the systems, scripts, sample letters, general costings, tools, apps, software and websites that you need to move forward. Each chapter will introduce you to a new facet of the knowledge necessary to starting a business in this sector, with lots of tips along the way. Wherever possible the book is action-oriented, and I suggest tasks that will support you in applying the information presented. As you progress through the book, I recommend you note down key learning points and ideas, and always monitor the most up-to-date information provided by the government and the NHS.

Let's get started.

CHAPTER 1

The Care Industry

What kind of business is a care agency? In this chapter, we will explore what a care agency is, the different forms it can take and what kind of work it entails.

By the end of this chapter, you should have a good understanding of:

- The care industry, the work it involves and the opportunities that exist within it

- What a care agency looks like and the different types of care available

- The differences between domiciliary care and supported living

- The business opportunities that exist in care

- The various elements that you should consider when setting up a business in the care sector

Why the care sector?

No matter what business you're in, you need to have a powerful reason why you are doing it – 'to make money' is not enough, particularly in the care sector. Working in a care business can be challenging. On tough days (and there will be many of these) when the mundane but essential tasks are pressing – such as making that sales call, dropping those leaflets or sending out another load of repetitive sales emails – your 'why' is what keeps you going, because only you can see the bigger picture, giving you the energy to push through.

You can have one 'why' or many. Examples are 'I hate my current job', 'I want to improve my family's life', or maybe you have had a personal experience with the care sector that is motivating you. The 'why' must be personal and there is no right or wrong answer.

What is a care agency?

A care agency is an organisation – public or private – that is primarily engaged in providing skilled or professional care, treatment and support to individuals, their families and carers. This care, treatment and support can be provided in residential accommodation, which is usually in a non-hospital setting, such as private care homes, hospices, shelters or supported living services. Care agencies can take various forms, but the main two are home care and supported living.

Home care versus supported living

Home care, also known as domiciliary care, is one of the largest sectors in the care industry, and the 'front line' of social care delivery. Domiciliary care is provided to people who still live in their own homes but require additional support with activities such as household tasks, personal care and any other tasks to enable them to maintain their independence and quality of life.

Supported living is a service designed to help people with a wide range of support needs to retain their independence by providing support in a residential home that is often shared with other like-minded individuals and will typically have 24-hour staff on site.

It is important to differentiate between domiciliary care and supported living because they are very different types of care provision. With domiciliary care, the clients continue to live in their own homes, whether that's a property they own or rent, or one they live in with family. By contrast, a supported living home is a residence designed to be shared with individuals requiring similar levels and types of support. It is important to note that supported living homes are not considered care homes or nursing homes and so are not inspected by the Care Quality Commission (CQC). These homes are deemed to be the clients' own homes, as they involve a tenancy agreement held directly between the tenant and the landlord.

Other types of care agency include residential care homes and nursing homes, which have a similar set-up to supported living, except that the homes in these cases are not regarded as the tenants' own homes; rather, they are residents of the home. These types of home often have more restrictions placed on them and will also be inspected by the CQC. (This level of restrictions does not apply to care businesses not regulated by the CQC, such as homes for 16–18-year-olds who do not require personal care.)

Before setting up your care business, you will need to decide the target audience you wish to serve, the type and level of services you will be providing (eg elderly clients, children, adults with learning disabilities, etc) and where and how you will provide these services. Think about the different types of care services you are able to supply, how these fit into your business model and how you can provide quality care in the best possible way.

The business opportunity

The United Kingdom Homecare Association (UKHCA) estimates that around 249 million hours of home care are delivered in England each year.[1] The care industry is constantly evolving and, as it does so, more and more business opportunities arise.

---

1   J Holmes (2016). 'An overview of the domiciliary care market in the United Kingdom', United Kingdom Homecare Association website. Available at: www.ukhca.co.uk/downloads.aspx?ID=109

In 2015, more than 350,000 older people in England were estimated to use home care services, 257,000 of whom had their care paid for by their local authority. A further 76,300 younger people with learning disabilities, physical disabilities or mental health problems were also estimated to be using publicly funded home care.[2] These represent substantial numbers of people requiring different forms of care, which is indicative of how important the domiciliary care market is in the delivery of care. Those needing care is set to rise further as people live longer and more of us require care in the community, and the demand for mental health support is similarly increasing.

Over the past two years, three of the biggest national providers of home care (Saga Care UK, and Housing 21) have withdrawn from the publicly funded home care market, while two others (Mears and Mitie) reported losses in their home care divisions. Mitie subsequently sold its home care business for just £2.[3]

Currently over 950,000 adults in the UK receive home-based care,[4] and the domiciliary care industry is currently worth approximately £5 billion per year.[5] There are more

---

2   R Wittenberg and B Hu (2015). 'Projections of demand for and costs of social care for older people and young adults in England, 2015 to 2035', PSSRU discussion paper No 2900. London School of Economics and Political Science. Available at: www.pssru.ac.uk/publications/pub-4992
3   (2017) 'Mitie sells home care business for £2', BBC News. Available at: www.bbc.co.uk/news/business-39126019
4   National Audit Office (2021). 'The adult social care market in England', Department of Health & Social Care. Available at: www.nao.org.uk/wp-content/uploads/2021/03/The-adult-social-care-market-in-England.pdf
5   'Domiciliary care in the UK statistics', Ibisworld. Available at: www.ibisworld.com/united-kingdom/market-research-reports/domiciliary-care-industry/

than 10,000 homecare providers in England registered with the CQC, with the Department of Health & Social Care (DHSC) predicting that 57% more adults over 65 will require care over the next 15 years.[6]

What does all this data mean, and what is the opportunity for those seeking to build a successful business in this sector? The care industry is evolving rapidly and the departure of larger healthcare companies creates a vacuum that needs to be filled, providing opportunities for newcomers.

From a financial perspective, the level of income that can be created from running a successful care business will depend on how quickly you scale up and how large you want your organisation to be. The beauty of the care industry is that even smaller businesses can do well financially. You don't need to be a vast organisation with endless resources and hundreds of staff to be hugely successful in this sector.

The care sector has many facets and so there are numerous business avenues you can take and a wide variety of specialties, all of which can be lucrative businesses if you adopt the right approach and systems. Examples of businesses within the care industry include:

---

6   'Homecare facts and figures: number of providers, service users and workforce', Homecare.co.uk. Available at: www.homecare.co.uk/advice/home-care-facts-and-stats-number-of-providers-service-users-workforce

- Domiciliary care
- Respite
- Recruitment agency
- Training company
- PPE supplier
- Professional services/consultancy
- Residential home/nursing home
- Children's home
- Supported living

In this book we focus on domiciliary care agencies and supported living services, which are CQC-regulated businesses. (The set-up processes for nursing and residential care agencies are quite different to that for domiciliary care and supported living, though they are also CQC regulated.)

Between 2016 and 2017, the CQC registered 8,500 domiciliary care services. Every quarter, at least 500 agencies register with the CQC – quite a sizeable figure; however, data illustrates that an almost equal number, around 400 agencies, deregister in the same period.[7]

---

7   L Jefferson et al (2018). 'Home Care in England: Views from the commissioners and providers'. The King's Fund. Available at: www.kingsfund.org.uk/sites/default/files/2018-12/Home-care-in-England-report.pdf

Many of these agencies deregister before they have even begun to offer any services.

This rate of deregistration may seem alarming, but there are many reasons as to why a care business doesn't work out and they take the costly steps of deregistering. Understanding what makes a successful agency is important, as is being able to recognise a failing one, so that you can avoid this and stay on the path to success.

Some of the biggest challenges that new care businesses face include:

- A lack of clients

- Insufficient funding

- Poor or absent marketing strategy

- Inadequate operations

In the following chapters, we will look at the elements of a good, profitable care business, walking you through what's involved to give you the best chance of success.

Task

- Earlier I mentioned that it is important to set your 'why', as this helps to shape your goals. Get a pinboard and some pins. Then, sit in a quiet place and start thinking about the life you want – this is your 'why'.

Search online and in magazines for images that represent those dreams and the life that you want to create and use them to create a vision board. Place this somewhere you will see it every day so that it will provide daily inspiration to keep you on track as you work through this book and toward building a successful care business.

- Decide on the kind of care business you want to operate, for example whether you intend to offer domiciliary care or a supported living service. We will explore what these involve in more detail later on, but for now think about whether you like the idea of supporting people in their own homes or would rather provide support in one location.

- Decide what kind of clients you wish to serve – for example will you specialise in care of the elderly, adult mental health, children, or those with dementia? To start with, I would suggest you work with a group that you are familiar with, whether that's through your work or personal experience. A familiarity will make things easier, but is not essential – I started out working with adults with learning disabilities with no prior experience – it will just be a steeper learning curve.

CHAPTER 2

Setting Up Your Company

When setting up your care business, it is important to understand the different company structures and how and why the organisation of a care company matters. The legalities and registration of companies will differ from country to country – in this book we will only be covering how UK companies are set up.

This chapter will enable you to:

- Recognise different company structures in the UK and the differences between them

- Understand the importance of developing a brand and business name

Company structures

It is important to choose the right structure for your care business to enable it to function effectively. Seek out professional advice before making key decisions. In the UK, there are three main types of company structure:

1. Limited company

2. Sole trader

3. Partnership

Limited Company

In a limited company, the business exists as a separate legal entity and must be registered with Companies House. This means that the individuals involved in the business, such as shareholders (owners) and directors (managers), are separate from the business. The business can enter into contracts and be sued for breaching them. If this happens, the directors' and/or shareholders' personal assets cannot be seized to pay off debts, so this business structure offers some protection. The downside, though, is that there are certain restrictions and rules that must be followed as to how you operate the company (particularly if you are not the main shareholder).

Sole trader

A sole trader is effectively a one-man band, a business owned and operated by just one individual. The main advantage of this business structure is that sole traders have a lot of control over their business, profits and assets. It is a straightforward and flexible way to operate a business. Unlike a limited company, however, sole traders are personally liable for any debts the business accrues and personal assets can be seized to settle those debts, so the greater freedom and control comes with a higher level of risk.

Partnership

In a traditional partnership, you and your business partner(s) own the business and are jointly responsible for any liabilities. With a partnership there is no need to register at Companies House. Instead, you draw up a partnership agreement between you that clearly identifies the business structure and the roles and responsibilities of those involved. Partnerships can be more tax efficient than operating as a sole trader or a limited company, though this will depend on individual circumstances. It is important to remember, however, that partners will be held personally liable for the business's debts in the same way that a sole trader is.

This book will focus on sole traders and limited companies and the differences between them, as partnerships commonly operate in a similar fashion to sole traders.

Choosing a name

One of the first decisions you'll make about your business is its name. This is an important choice, as it is often the first impression a customer gets of your business. If you get it right, your business name will help you stand out to potential investors and clients. Those who decide to go down the limited company route will need to check that no one else has the same or a similar business name registered at Companies House. You can do this on the Companies House website (www.gov.uk/government/organisations/companies-house).

In today's digital world, a website is essential. This should be a factor in your business name decision, as you need to ensure the domain name you want isn't already owned by someone else. There are multiple sites where you can check available domain names and possible alternatives or variations.

As well as a website, your business also needs a social media presence. To help your potential customers find you easily, your social media handles should be the same as or as close as possible to your business name, so also check these are available before you make your final name decision. To simplify this task, you can use an online tool to check the availability of a handle across all social media platforms.[8]

---

8   For example, try www.namechk.com

Task

To start you on your journey to setting up your care business:

- Seek professional advice as to the best business structure for your company

- Come up with a list of potential company names

- Check Companies House to see if any of these are already registered businesses and cross them off your list (if you are registering as a limited company)

- For the names you have left, check whether the obvious domain names and social media handles are available and, if not, if there are close alternatives

- Review your list to identify the name that will enable you to build the strongest and most identifiable business across multiple online platforms

CHAPTER 3

Your Business Plan

Your business plan is an important document that maps out your key ideas for and basic components of your business. It is essentially a strategy that outlines how your business will operate, what resources you will need, and the products and services you intend to offer to your customers. You should never outsource the writing of your business plan – you are the only person who can truly understand your ambitions and goals, which is what the business plan should communicate, so this must come from you.

After reading this chapter you should have a good understanding of:

- What a business plan is and why you need one

- How to write a detailed business plan and what should be included

- What information you will need to collect and prepare for your business plan

- The importance of your mission and vision

- What a SWOT analysis is, why you need to do one and how to create one for your business

- How a marketing strategy fits into your business plan

- How to map out your operations strategy

- The best ways to identify potential funding sources and other resources you will need for your care business

What is a business plan?

A business plan is a strategic document that carefully details the framework on which your business will be built. More specifically, it is designed to identify, describe and analyse either a potential business opportunity or your existing business, evaluating its viability in terms of resources and financials. It is also one of the documents that the CQC will ask for as part of your application and, in some cases, you will be asked to explain and justify your plan, making it even more important that you have written your own business plan and understand it inside out.

Next we discuss the different sections your business plan should contain and what's included in each of these. These sections are:

- Mission and vision

- Market research

- SWOT analysis

- Marketing

- Funding/cashflow forecast

- Operations

Mission and vision

In your business plan, communicate the values you are trying to promote in your business, what is driving you and your unique selling point(s) (USPs), along with an introduction to your business and why it is needed in the context of what is already out there.

Your business plan should include a mission and/or a vision statement, a statement about who you are and what you plan to do, now and into the future. Even when an organisation changes its strategy or approach, its mission and vision will typically remain the same.

A **mission statement** should define your business's objectives and purpose. It should be written in the present tense and map out the 'why' behind your business. Why do you do what you do? Mission statements should always be clear and concise.

A **vision statement** also relates to your purpose but it will focus more on the goals and aspirations for what you want to achieve out in the world; it is more outward-facing and forward-looking than your mission, which is often more personal.

The mission and/or vision statement start the introduction to your business plan and demonstrate the ideas that are at the heart of your company. Following these statements should be an introductory section that enables the reader to learn more about your business and why you are different from your competitors. Be careful what you say in your introduction: don't make promises that you can't keep or commit to something unrealistic that you may fail to deliver. When setting the scene for your business you must be realistic, relatable and believable, taking into account your level of resources and experience. The introduction is where you should talk about what client needs your business intends to meet and how; in other words, what gap you have identified in the market and how you expect to fill it. What's more, you should explain how you will do this better than your competitors.

Your business plan should also include a bit about yourself, specifically your work history and experience in the sector you'll be operating in and your anticipated role in the company.

Market research

Before launching any business, it's important to thoroughly research and study the market to identify gaps and client needs. It's essential that you can identify your market, potential clients and competitors. This will establish that there is a need for the service or product you are bringing to the market, potential clients out there willing to pay for it, and that they are not being adequately or completely served by the existing service providers.

At this stage of the book, I expect that you know who your clientele will be – the elderly, children, adults with learning disabilities, for example. Now you need to study businesses that are catering for this same group of clients. When I started my care business, I identified other providers and called them up to discuss a fictitious potential client; I asked lots of questions about their service and also visited a number of them. This gave me insight into how different businesses operated and enabled me to identify what I believed I could do better, things I would avoid and, more importantly, any service gaps that I couldn't fill.

In the care sector, you also need to research the geographic area in which you intend to operate to find out what types of care are over- or under-provided and the gaps in the market, to ensure sufficient work for your business. For example, some areas may have many agencies specialising in elderly care, but a shortage of those working with learning disabilities or mental health. Taking the time to gather this knowledge early on will ensure you start on the right track, and including this information in your business plan demonstrates a solid understanding of the sector and of your business's place in it, both to potential investors and to CQC inspectors.

SWOT analysis

Armed with your market research, you should carry out a SWOT analysis. This will give you an in-depth understanding of your competitors, highlight your strengths and weaknesses and identify the business opportunities that arise from these, as well as the potential risks involved and threats to your business. If you have been thorough in your market research, you should have all the information you need for your SWOT analysis.

A SWOT analysis has four segments, each with some questions to ask yourself.

When carrying out your SWOT analysis, it is important to be objective. It might be helpful to ask others for their opinion. Honesty is essential to a good SWOT analysis, whether it's for personal or business purposes. This means not shying away from admitting faults and weaknesses, while also recognising strengths.

Strengths

- What are your natural skills?

- What other skills have you gained and developed?

- What are your natural gifts or talents?

- What experience do you have in the industry?

- Do you already have a business in the industry that could enhance your potential care company?

Weaknesses

- Do you have any negative work habits or traits?

- Do you need improvement in any area of training or education?

- What would other people see as your weaknesses?

Opportunities

- What is the economic situation in your industry?

- What is currently lacking in the industry that you think you can provide?

- What opportunities for growth are there?

- Is your industry growing or struggling?

- Is there a new or emerging technology or innovation you could adopt as your USP?

Threats

- Is your industry changing direction or contracting?

- Is competition strong in the sector you want to target?

- What do you see as the biggest external danger to your business's progression?

When you have completed the exercise, you can set about turning negatives into positives, weaknesses into strengths, threats into opportunities. This might necessitate further education or extra qualifications, but this will be in service of meeting your business goals and increasing your chances of success.

Marketing

Marketing is how you intend to source and secure clients, the approach or strategy you are going to use to get your business out there and start winning contracts and generating revenue.

Marketing is fundamental to your success because the lifeline of any business is its clients, so you need a clear plan of how you intend to attract clients. What your marketing strategy will look like is something to think about early on in your business journey. Do not make the mistake of thinking you have time to worry about marketing once the business is up and running or once you have your license. Working out exactly how you will get clients should be one of your first major tasks and be clearly explained in your business plan.

As a first step to developing your strategy, identify your target audience, where they are and how you can reach them. Often, people who have worked in the care industry assume clients will simply be referred to them because of their contacts, connections and prior experience. However, many of these experienced care workers find themselves left out in the cold once they become business owners in this sector. The only way to guarantee that you will get clients is to assume you are starting from nothing, that you have no connections in the industry. This way, anything else is a bonus.

The marketing strategy section of your business plan should discuss:

- The marketing techniques and strategies that you will be using, whether traditional, digital or a combination of both – this could be flyers, online advertising or use of a marketing platform such as HomeCare (www.homecare.co.uk) or Care Sourcer

- How often you will run marketing campaigns

- How often you will review your marketing strategy

- What metrics you will track and review to evaluate the success of your strategy

Funding/cashflow forecast

An important section of your business plan is where you explain what funding you will need to launch and operate your business and where this will come from. Without funding, any business will eventually collapse. For a business to thrive, healthy financials are essential.

'Healthy' here means having enough money to fund research and development and marketing in addition to the usual business expenses such as rent, salaries, professional subscriptions and so on. And of course, a successful business should be making a profit – this is particularly important if you have shareholders, as they will expect to see a return on their investment. To ensure you can remain in a healthy financial situation, a good understanding and management of your cash flow is crucial from the outset, and this is another thing that the CQC will quiz you about before they grant you your license.

Healthy cash flow can only be achieved with careful and thorough planning. One of the biggest challenges faced by new companies in the care sector, before they have even been issued a licence, is the cost of launching and developing the business. New care companies also face a huge challenge in the form of late payments, as local authorities are particularly notorious for this – they can take up to three or four months to pay an invoice, which can put a lot of additional pressure on a new company if cash flow is tight. For this reason, I would advise you to ensure you start out with a cushion, a reserve fund that will be able to keep you going until your first invoice is paid – bearing in mind that this might be later than you expect.

Before you can even apply for your licence, let alone start looking for clients, you will need to get various things set up and in place ready for opening your business, much of which will incur an upfront cost. A list and assessment of these costs should be included in the financials section of your business plan. In the care industry, typical set-up costs include:

- Premises (rent and possibly fixtures and fittings)

- Overheads such as utilities, water, telephone usage and business rates

- Equipment, materials and resources

- Staff recruitment

- Staff training

- Marketing

- Subscriptions, eg for computer systems

- Licences and accreditations

Operations

Your mission and vision explain where your business is going; your business operations are how you will get there. This section of the plan explains how your business will operate and the systems, processes and policies that will support it. It should highlight what resources you already have, what you need and what staff you need to recruit.

For any business to function effectively, deliver on its promises and achieve its objectives, it needs smooth and efficient operations behind the scenes. This involves developing fail-proof systems that everyone in the organisation understands and abides by. In the care industry, this is particularly important because you are dealing with vulnerable people, so you cannot let things fall by the wayside or allow standards to slip.

Premises

There are many things you need to consider that fall under the broad umbrella of 'operations'. First and foremost, though, is where your business will operate from – the location and the premises. No matter what type of office (home office, rented space, shared office) you decide to work from, you will need it, as a minimum, to be:

- Safe and secure

- Accessible

- Have adequate fire alarms and exits

- Have business insurance

- Include lockable and separate spaces for private conversations

- Contain suitable locations for files to be locked away or held on a secure server

Staff and structure

Staff are a key element of any organisation and crucial to a business's success. Often, they are regarded as the heart of an organisation as without them a company will collapse. To maintain harmony and order, especially where you have a sizeable team, a clear organisational structure is crucial. This provides direct reporting lines and sets out each person's role, responsibilities and tasks within the organisation, which removes ambiguity and duplication of effort.

When working out your organisational structure in regard to staffing, consider:

- How big will your team need to be?

- How will you structure the team – what and how many roles will there be, and what reporting structure will be used?

- Recruitment and selection – do you want to use one clear repeatable programme for staff at all levels, or are you looking for different skills/traits for different roles?

- How will you structure staff training and development?

Systems

What systems will be required to run the business efficiently? In the care industry, there are a multitude of systems required to ensure you and your team are on top of the extensive paperwork and legalities involved in this sector.

Many new companies are daunted by this and rush out to buy digital systems to keep track of all this and remain compliant. These aren't always necessary. A system that is clear and easy for all to understand and comply with is just as efficient as a digital one. There is something to be said, however, for having your business go digital early on so that the growth process and progress occur more smoothly. For this reason, while I don't recommend you purchase every digital system going, some that will make your life easier in this industry are those for staff rota planning, email systems and software, care plan notes, compliance checking and records management.

Policies

In the care industry, policies are what guide your staff on how to handle any issues that arise in day-to-day operations. Policies detail how each and every scenario should be dealt with so that staff and service users have a reference point or a benchmark. Policies can be written by you or you could employ the services of organisations who specialise in policy writing.

When thinking about your policies, consider:

- What kinds of policies and procedures will you need, and who will develop them?

- How will staff be informed of these policies?

- How often will the policies be reviewed and updated, and by whom?

Examples of policies that you will likely need to create include:

- Complaints

- Care plans

- Safeguarding

- Compliance

- Bullying

- Recruitment

Compliance

One of your policies will be about compliance, an area that warrants a more detailed discussion. The nature of this industry, and the huge responsibility you have in supporting vulnerable people, makes it imperative that all information is accurately recorded. The care industry is heavily regulated, following multiple incidents of abuse having been identified in a variety of care industry settings. The global coronavirus pandemic has added further layers of regulation and monitoring.

A comprehensive compliance policy and process will ensure you utilise a systematic and consistent method to monitor what is going on in your organisation. This can be paper-based or digital; either approach is acceptable, provided information is recorded regularly and accurately, and any learnings evaluated and acted upon.

Your compliance policy should detail:

- How regulatory requirements will be monitored
- Where and how incidents are reported
- Who will deal with compliance issues
- How often compliance will be reviewed and by whom

Task

Start your business plan by developing your mission and vision.

Development of mission:

- First, identify the 'big idea' that underlies your business, something powerful that helps to differentiate you from your competition. What is your USP? Why should customers choose you?

- Next, think about your goals. What metrics can you use to track your progress toward achieving them?

Development of vision:

- First, identify the purpose behind your organisation, or the factors that drive it. What is the problem that your business solves? How does it make life easier or better for your customers?

- Next, define your value. What will customers value about your business?

CHAPTER 4

The CQC Registration Process

Registering your care business with the CQC can be a daunting process and, in some cases, a lengthy one, depending on the kind of service you wish to register. In this chapter, we will go through the process of applying for CQC registration and the initial application form.

Ideally, you will have all the documentation you need ready before submission so that the process will be smooth. Even so, there is a strong possibility the CQC will come back to you to ask for more information. The submission process requires you not only to complete an application form but also provide a number of supporting documents, so preparation is key. The application process itself can also occur in multiple stages, depending on the kind of service you are applying for a licence to operate.

By the end of this chapter, you will:

- Know what the CQC is and its role in establishing and running a care business

- Understand what a regulated activity is

- Be able to put together a CQC checklist for your business

- Identify the relevant people to appoint within your organisation, as required under CQC registration

- Be able to collate supporting evidence for your application

Understanding the Care Quality Commission (CQC)

The CQC is an independent body responsible for health and social care in England. The role of the CQC is to ensure health and social care services are providing people with safe, effective, compassionate and high-quality care, as well as to encourage and support care providers on how they can improve and provide the best possible service. To achieve this, the CQC monitor, inspect and regulate service providers to ensure they meet defined standards of quality and safety.

The results of the inspections, along with associated care provider ratings, are published on the CQC website. This applies to both public and private sector companies. This allows potential clients to find out how you are rated by the authorities and can be a deciding factor for clients when they are choosing which service to use. Not all care providers need to be registered with the CQC, only those who will be providing a regulated activity. Often, though, local authorities will only use a service with a CQC rating.

What is a regulated activity? In the care sector, the provision of personal care for people who are unable to provide it for themselves for reasons such as old age, illness or disability is a regulated activity. For the purposes of this book, I will assume that you intend to provide a regulated activity and therefore will need to register with the CQC. This remains useful information, though, even if you don't intend to provide personal care to your clients.

CQC checklist

In addition to the CQC application, you will need to prepare and submit a range of supporting documents to back up your application. These include:

- A Registered Manager's application form, including a personal statement

- A statement of your vision and mission for the business, along with your experience

- Details of the Nominated Individual (see below)

- A Statement of Purpose, which must be person-centred

- Sample care plans

- Your business plan and financial information

- A business continuity plan

- The policies and procedures that will govern your care business

- If your business will provide supported living, then floor plans and sample tenancy agreements are also needed

The Registered Manager and Nominated Individual

It is essential that you understand the roles and responsibilities of each member of your team and how these fit into the wider business strategy. This is especially important with regards to the senior team roles in CQC-regulated agencies. Within the care sector, there are two main roles that are mandatory to run a regulated care agency, but essential for any care business. The roles are:

- Registered Manager (RM)

- Nominated Individual (NI)

Both positions must be filled by qualified individuals experienced in their respective fields. This is key to ensure the smooth operation of the business. In some cases, the Nominated Individual and Registered Manager will be the same person; in others, they will be two separate hires (if you're not taking on one of these roles yourself). Either scenario is fine. It is imperative that you have the right people in place to enable the seamless operation of your business at all levels, from management through to supervisors and support staff.

The role of the Registered Manager

The Health and Social Care Act 2008, in Regulation 7, states that registered providers must have a Registered Manager.[9] Registering your Registered Manager is a separate application to the registration of your service (the business). Their application is based on their character and the licence they are ultimately issued with is associated with their name, rather than the business they are working for. Thus, it is imperative that they are supported by the organisation they work for, as they can be held liable for the things that go wrong with the service, such as any safeguarding issues or negligence that occurs while under their watch. This is an important role in the care business, as they carry ultimate responsibility.

As mentioned, the Registered Manager can also be the Nominated Individual but this individual would need to complete the application and interview process for both roles. This dual role is often the case where the business

---

9   'Regulation 7: Requirements relating to registered managers'. Available at: www. cqc.org.uk/guidance-providers/regulations-enforcement/regulation-7-requirements-relating-registered-managers

is a small organisation and, for example, the owner of the business also wishes to manage it.

According to Regulation 5 of the Health and Social Care Act, the Registered Manager must:[10]

- Be of good character

- Be able to demonstrate the ability to properly perform tasks that are intrinsic to their role

- Possess the necessary qualifications, competence, skills and experience to manage all regulated activity

- Provide documents that confirm their suitability

This provision of the Act seeks to ensure that those who are responsible for the organisation are fit and suitable for the role of running the organisation; this applies to both the Nominated Individual and Registered Manager.

Supporting evidence

The role of the Registered Manager is crucial because of the responsibility they have towards service users. As such, the CQC requires that they provide evidence of their experience and demonstrate they understand the importance and responsibility of their position. The

---

10 'Fit and proper persons: directors'. Available at: www.cqc.org.uk/guidance-providers/regulations-enforcement/fit-proper-persons-directors

supporting evidence that is required to support their application includes:

- A brief summary of their professional experience and specialisms

- Qualifications illustrating suitable candidacy for the role of Registered Manager (managers must have, as a minimum, a level 3 NVQ (National Vocational Qualification) and be working towards a level 5 NVQ)

- Previous work references, ID documentation, enhanced DBS (Disclosure and Barring Service) check

- Letter from GP confirming fitness to work

The application can be submitted online (this is the preferred method) or using a Word document that can be downloaded from the CQC website.[11]

The Nominated Individual

The role of the Nominated Individual is to oversee the day-to-day running of the organisation. Like the Registered Manager, they will need to demonstrate that they have the relevant experience and qualifications to handle running an organisation.

---

11   'Apply as a new registered manager'. Available at: www.cqc.org.uk/guidance-providers/registration/registered-manager-application/apply-new-registered-manager

Examples of what would be considered an acceptable demonstration of experience include:

- Having previously run a company

- Expertise in financial management

- Marketing skills

- Governance and compliance understanding and ability

In some cases, a Nominated Individual may not have all the necessary experience; in this case, the CQC requires them to demonstrate how they can acquire or access this expertise, for example by hiring qualified team members or having consultants on hand who can provide the required expertise, for example an accountant to act as financial advisor, HR consultant to manage HR issues, and so on.

People often assume that the Nominated Individual will require a care background or experience – this is not the case. For example, in my own case, I came from a property background. I had no experience in care but a wealth of knowledge of starting and running successful businesses. What the CQC is looking for is evidence that you have experience of running an organisation successfully. What they are trying to avoid, as much as possible, is care agencies opening and closing because of poor management. This is a concern because, unlike other businesses, when a care business fails, the lives of vulnerable people are at stake.

As such, the CQC require you to demonstrate that you are sufficiently competent to make the business a success.

Task

- Begin gathering the documentation you will need to submit with your CQC application

- Decide who your RM and NI will be, identify their qualifications and experience and begin to collate the documentation and evidence to support this

- Identify any gaps in experience for these individuals and plan how you will fill these

CHAPTER 5

The CQC Application

In this chapter, we will go through the different steps of completing the CQC application form, a major part of the process of obtaining a licence and setting up your care business. The application form will request a lot of the information discussed in previous chapters, such as whether you are registering as an organisation, a sole trader or a partnership, so it's important that you have fully thought through how your business will be structured and the way you intend to operate before you start the application form.

It is also critical that, before you start the application process, you have a good understanding of the care business, how it operates, the resources you will need and the policies and systems that must be implemented to ensure the seamless day-to-day operations of the business, regardless of which area you specialise in.

By the end of this chapter, you should understand:

- What information will be requested in the first part of the application form and how to complete this section

- What is meant by Key Lines of Enquiry (KLOEs) and be able to complete this section fully and accurately

- The importance of data protection and keeping client and employee data safe and secure

- The value of financial management

- What policies you must prepare and present to the CQC

- The supporting documents you'll be required to submit alongside your application

The first half of the CQC application form, which can be obtained online on the CQC website (cqc.org.uk), covers the basics about your organisation and who will be running it, such as:

- The name of the service

- The location of the service

- Details of the RM

- Details of the NI

- The Key Lines of Enquiry (KLOEs)

Most of these sections are easy to complete as they are relatively straightforward, but some warrant a more detailed discussion. Remember that although you need to provide details of the Registered Manager in this part of the application, they will need to complete a separate application of their own, which can only be emailed to the manager once the main form is complete. The information you provide at this point will automatically save and prepopulate the Registered Manager's form. We will explore what's needed for the Registered Manager's form in more detail in the next chapter.

KLOEs

The Key Lines of Enquiry (KLOEs) are prompts and sources of evidence that you, as a provider, need to ensure you have in your service. These will come up both in your application and in your interview, and again during the CQC inspections once your service is up and running.

There are five KLOEs that you will need to provide evidence for in the application:

1. Safe
2. Effective
3. Caring
4. Responsive
5. Well-led

Safe

The first key line of enquiry is looking for a demonstration that your organisation will maintain the highest standards of safety when caring for vulnerable people. This needs to be reflected right across the organisation. How can you demonstrate that your organisation will meet the criteria to be regarded as 'safe'?

Below are a series of questions which, when answered fully, will enable you to understand and demonstrate how you will keep your service users safe. These are the types of questions the CQC are likely to ask. Your answers should be properly thought through and backed up with evidence.

- How will you protect service users from abuse while they are under your care?

- What systems and processes will be in place to report incidents and accidents?

- What procedures do you have in place to investigate these?

- How will you ensure that there is an adequate supply of staff to meet requirements?

- How will you verify the skills and experience of staff members?

- How will you collect feedback from staff, service users and their families?

- What will you do with feedback to facilitate service improvement?

- What policies and procedures do you have in place for risk management?

- What policies and processes exist for infection control, for example in regard to coronavirus?

- Do you have a crisis response plan? What happens if things go wrong?

- What policies exist for staff training?

- How will training and development be accessed and delivered?

For each of the above areas you should provide practical examples of how you intend to address each question and, where applicable, give real-life examples of how you have provided this in a practical setting, such as in your previous care positions. Ultimately, this is about describing how you will deliver care safely to your clients.

Effective

This KLOE is about maintaining effectiveness in service provision, with a focus on constant and never-ending improvement. How will your business operate so that constant improvement is placed at its core? It is asking you to demonstrate how your organisation will run efficiently. What systems will you be setting up to ensure your organisation can run smoothly and, where there are problems, what systems will be in place that your staff can rely on? You can demonstrate that your service will be effective by answering the following questions – again, these are questions the CQC could ask – and supporting your answer with relevant evidence:

- How will you carry out assessments and deliver effective, evidence-based treatments?

- How will you ensure that every member of staff has the right level of skill, experience and competency to deliver the high standard of care that is required?

- How will you understand the needs of your service users? This could be by identifying their nutrition or hydration requirements and respecting cultural/religious needs, for example.

- How will you support clients to live healthier lives?

- How will you encourage participation in external activities or provide access to professionals when needed?

- How will your teams work with service users, other organisations and professionals (eg, in multidisciplinary teams)?

- How accessible is your building? Can staff, visitors and family members come and talk to you in the office (is it wheelchair friendly, easy to reach)?

- Will you involve service users in their care planning, for example by ensuring staff understand consent for care and treatment to ensure it can be delivered effectively?

- Will you conduct regular audit checks to monitor effectiveness and, where needed, take steps to initiate improvements?

- Are all systems and processes easily understood, readily accessible and is there sufficient training on these?

- Will you regularly obtain feedback from service users and families and work on improving on any issues raised? How will you demonstrate this?

- What policies do you have in place? Are these current and how will you communicate policy information to staff and service users?

Caring

This KLOE is about inclusive care, where service users are able to shape the care they receive and be involved in the decision-making process related to their treatment. Providing inclusive care involves looking closely at how you can include service users in the management of their care.

The CQC are looking for evidence of how your organisation will demonstrate compassion, empathy and an all-round inclusive service. You need to demonstrate how you intend to consider the service users' desires, needs, characteristics, religious beliefs and cultural practices and incorporate these into any care and treatment they receive. You need to show that the people you will be caring for are at the centre of the plan that is created for them and that their care plans will be continually adapted to suit changing needs.

You can create care plans that are person-centred by ensuring that the service user is involved in their care from the outset – from the initial assessment and care planning through to ongoing care delivery. Service users must be involved as much as possible throughout the process so that they receive care that is personal to them, where their wishes are respected as well as their care needs being met. Consider the following questions:

- How do you intend to collect feedback from service users and their families, and obtain input from other professionals involved in their care?

- How will you ensure that you respect their wishes, cultural beliefs, religious beliefs, sexuality etc?

- How can you find innovative ways to deliver care that is personal to service users who are particularly vulnerable? For example, adults with learning disabilities, non-verbal communicators, the elderly (perhaps with memory loss) or those with poor mental health?

- How will you ensure that you are able to deliver care that is personal to individuals who may not be able to express themselves fully or adequately?

- How do you intend to ensure service users always retain their dignity and privacy?

Responsive

You also need to demonstrate that your service can respond to the changing needs of the people you'll be caring for and that you can do this both easily and in a timely manner. The needs of those people will change, sometimes over a period of time, sometimes quite suddenly; the CQC want evidence that you can adapt to these changes quickly.

How can you demonstrate this? First, by actively seeking the views of your service users – what they would like to see changed, how they think the service can be improved, or even what you are doing well so that you can continue to do this. Then you can show how you will respond to the feedback that you receive and use this to provide person-centred care – feedback policies and processes are a good way of demonstrating this. You can decide and explain how often you will gather the views of service users, their family and other professionals and by what methods, such as feedback forms and group participation meetings.

As well as positive and constructive feedback, you may receive negative feedback and/or complaints. Part of being responsive will be effective handling of complaints

– dealing with them quickly, taking any necessary actions and communicating with all concerned parties.

Similarly, you also need to consider your responsiveness to incidents – meaning how quickly incidents are followed up, how any lessons learned are implemented and, where training is necessary, how quickly this is arranged and any required disciplinary action is taken.

Explain what systems you will have in place that mean you can be receptive to change and adapt quickly when needed, for example when dealing with a service user who is at the end of their life. Often, changes can relate to legislation – how will you keep up to date with these and adapt your service? This is particularly important in light of the global coronavirus pandemic.

Well-led

This KLOE segment is focused more on the senior management team – it looks at how well they run the organisation, how effectively and quickly information is passed down the organisation; how involved staff are in making decisions and in the growth of the organisation; how well your leadership monitors the organisation, in terms of growth and strategy but also in terms of ensuring both service users and staff feel protected by senior management. It also looks at fundamentals such as how the finances of the organisation are being managed. Finally, it examines how the management team ensures the company is delivering an excellent standard of care that is uniform across the organisation. Essentially, the focus of this KLOE is on the management team and how effective they are.

How can you demonstrate that you have effective management in place? Consider the following:

- How do you ensure that your staff understand the vision and mission of your organisation as well as of whom they are serving, plus the overall objectives of the organisation?

- How do you demonstrate effective communication throughout the organisation?

- How are changes communicated and how often does this happen?

- How involved are staff in making decisions for the organisation?

- How does management audit the services to provide continuous improvement? For example, addressing low staff turnover by conducting staff exit interviews to make improvements.

- Does the organisation establish good working relationships with other organisations to ensure effective and person-centred care for service users?

- How effective is the governance and strategy of the company?

- How does the company plan and track organisational growth?

- How efficient is the financial management of the organisation?

- How is ongoing support provided to staff, for example through training and development, ensuring equal access and treatment?

Data protection

The data protection section of the application is concerned with how you will monitor and safeguard the data of clients and staff. In recent years, this has become a particularly important concern for organisations in all industries. In the care sector, you must be even more zealous because of the sensitive nature of your clients' data.

GDPR regulations govern the way in which you can collect and store information about clients and employees and the procedures that you must follow in relation to data retention and deletion if asked. This topic will most likely be raised in your interview or, at the very least, your data protection policy will be one of the documents they ask for.

In order to satisfy the CQC's criteria with regard to data protection, you must do the following:

- Ensure that you provide consent forms that detail your privacy policies

- Ensure compliance when drafting contracts

- Check that your data protection and privacy policies are fit for purpose

- Implement strong security and governance processes for data management

- Provide staff training on GDPR

Financial viability

This section seeks to establish that your organisation is and will remain financially viable. Beyond the quality of actual care provided, this is one of the CQC's biggest concerns. As mentioned earlier, each year many care companies close because they run out of funds. This is often due to poor financial planning, for example because they haven't prepared a detailed plan that covers at least the first thirty-six months. In some cases, it's simply down to inexperience with and lack of understanding of the payment terms of local authority contracts. Often, new providers are dazzled by the amount of money they can make but don't take into account the significant ongoing costs that are incurred, as well as the initial expense of setting up the company and then keeping it ticking over until a paying client is secured, invoiced and then settles that invoice. Local authorities can take up to sixty days to pay an invoice after they have acknowledged receipt.

All of this needs to be factored into your business plan and you must ensure you have a sufficient cushion of funds to keep you going while you are establishing yourself. The CQC will want to see evidence that you have thought about cash flow and have made a contingency plan for how your business will run when things don't go according to plan. More specifically, they will ask for the following:

- An accountant who can verify liquidity

- Bank statements that show the business can be supported in the early days

- A financial forecast showing liquidity for the next twelve to eighteen months

- A business plan

- A cashflow forecast

- A business continuity plan for what you will do in cases of emergency, covering topics such as:

  - Storage and access of files if the office is inaccessible

  - Policies/processes in place in case of an emergency

  - How you communicate and keep in touch with staff

  - What happens if you have an outbreak of some kind, who staff will notify, when and what steps will be taken

 - Numbers to call/who to call in various
   emergency scenarios

Policies

The policies and procedures are documents you will need to create for your organisation. They are critically important as they act as your workplace bible. The policies and procedures are not there simply because CQC will ask for them but will dictate how your organisation operates.

Some organisations have hundreds of policies and procedures and some have less than thirty; either way, their purpose is to inform your team and others outside of your organisation how you operate. They provide a clear directory for queries should your staff, service users or their families have questions. Policies should always be easily accessible and available in an easy-to-read format as well as in braille, audio and multiple languages if you can afford to do so.

You can write your own policies if you feel confident enough, or you can hire a professional policy writer to draft them for you and to ensure they are tailored to the needs of your organisation. There are companies that can write these policies for you.

The CQC will ask you for several policies at the time of your application and they must all be presented as part of the registration and application process – failure to do so will inevitably delay your application. Delays are something you will wish to avoid as there is always a long waiting list to register new agencies.

It is imperative that you are familiar with your organisation's policies, especially those the CQC have specifically asked for, and have easy access to them so that there will be no delays if they ask you for these during the registration process. In some cases, local authorities will also ask to see your policies to ensure they are aligned with their own goals and objectives.

It is crucial that your policies are kept up to date, especially with the regular changes in legislation not least due to the pandemic but also because of the ongoing shake-up of the care industry. Any changes in policies should be immediately communicated to your team and your clients, especially where it directly impacts them. Where training is necessary due to a policy change, this should be acted upon immediately.

Supporting documents

Once you have completed the main application, you will need to provide several other supporting documents that help to make your application more robust and prepare you for the interview. These include:

DBS check. Specifically, you will be required to complete the enhanced DBS check, which is more thorough than the standard check and is usually completed via the Post Office. Note that this will take a week to two weeks to arrive and needs to be completed for both the Registered Manager and the Nominated Individual.

Business insurance. You must supply proof that you are covered by business insurance. I would recommend you shop around for this, as prices vary considerably. Top tip: you can obtain insurance in principle for the registration process, so that you don't incur any costs until you are fully operational.

ICO certificate. This is a legal requirement. Because you will be handling data related to both staff and clients, you will need to be registered with the Information Commissioner's Office (ICO) to legally process and store data. The cost of certification varies and is based on the size of the organisation, but prices start at £40. You can find out more on the ICO website.[12]

Sample care plans. The CQC will want to see what systems you have in place and how you will record client information, for example where you keep assessments, updates, notes, personal information, reports and staff updates. A sample care plan gives them a full picture of your systems and processes. These can be digital or paper-based, and the sample does not have to be a real client.

---

12   http://ico.org.uk

Your references. You will need to provide the details of your previous employers as well as a reference from your employer, or someone who can vouch for your suitability to provide the service. Again, this applies for both the Nominated Individual and the Registered Manager.

For supported living service applicants, you will also need to provide:

Floorplans. If you are putting in an application for supported living, you will need to submit floorplans of the property, as it will need to be inspected to ensure it is fit for purpose. Top tip: register your care agency first and then your supported living application later. This will reduce the registration period because waiting for an inspector to visit the premises will cause a delay; you want to avoid this, as there are more hoops to get through. Rather, focus first on ensuring your service meets the CQC standards – their main concern is that you are competent enough to run a care service that will deliver a regulated activity. Once you have obtained your licence, you can then simply log on to the CQC portal and apply to update your licence for a supported living service. Please note, however, this does not apply to services such as residential care homes and nursing homes, only supported living.

A tenancy agreement. This must be easy to read and must show that you, as the care provider, are not also the landlord of the property. If you have a separate property company that manages your supported living accommodation, this will be acceptable to CQC, but these companies must be separate entities.

Finally, you should also supply the Registered Manager's application.

This chapter has included a lot of detail, so I have set some tasks to help ensure you have grasped the major points.

Task

- Describe how you will deliver care effectively

- Describe how you will demonstrate the 'caring' principle

- Describe how your service will be responsive

- Describe how your service will be well-led

- Prepare a business continuity plan for your organisation

- Write a list of the policies you intend to use and decide whether you will draft these yourself or contract a professional to do so

- Collate all your supporting documentation in one place and identify any gaps

CHAPTER 6

Registered Manager's Application

As mentioned in the previous chapter, the application form for the Registered Manager is separate from the application form to register the service. The CQC wants to ensure that the person responsible for those under the service's care is both qualified and experienced enough to do the job successfully, because ultimately people's lives are at risk if they fail.

During your main CQC licence application you will have selected what kind of regulated activity you will be providing, for example personal care. The selection made when completing the provider's application form will be automatically pre-populated in the Registered Manager's application. The remainder of the application form consists of several sections, which we will go through in turn in this chapter.

General information

This section is broadly similar to the provider application form and asks for general details about the Registered Manager such as name, address and date of birth.

Details of management responsibilities

This section is asking for details on what exactly the role in the service will entail, ensuring the Registered Manager understands what their legal duty is and what is expected, for example:

- What it means to be responsible for the day-to-day running of the organisation

- Who the Registered Manager will be responsible for

- How the Registered Manager will ensure they manage the service responsibly

- What qualifies the Registered Manager to manage the service

- Broadly what skills the Registered Manager brings to the organisation

- Broadly what experience the Registered Manager brings to the role

Where the job of the Registered Manager is being shared, each manager will be required to complete an application and elaborate on what their areas of responsibility will be and what they bring to the table.

Skills and competencies

In this section, you will need to go into more detail about the skills possessed that mean the Registered Manager will be able to successfully perform their duties. This will include any training completed and skills acquired from past work experience.

DBS

Any individual working in the care industry is required to have an enhanced DBS check, because of the risk to the vulnerable people who are being supported. It is imperative that the people providing that support are appropriate and safe to do so.

Previous experience

This section is not simply about listing the various businesses previously worked within but about showcasing how the work has prepared the applicant for the role of Registered Manager of a care agency. They need to illustrate that the tasks and responsibilities in previous roles are relevant to this role and will enable them to perform it effectively.

It is important that a full history is provided, even if there are employment gaps. These should be acknowledged and explained – for example, gaps due to travelling, maternity or paternity leave. Any unexplained gaps in the timeline will more than likely prompt queries from the CQC. They will ask for your permission to contact previous employers to verify experience.

Previous registrations

The CQC will also want to know of any previous registrations with them. If you recall, we discussed that the licence for a Registered Manager is unique to the individual – it cannot be transferred from one person to another, or from one provider to another. Each time a Registered Manager leaves a service they must deregister themselves and then re-register in their new position.

There are a couple of reasons for this. First, it protects the Registered Manager from any incidents that take place in or allegations that are made about the service after they have left the organisation. This is important because any breach falls on the head of the Registered Manager; they are held personally liable for incidents that occur under their watch, so it is imperative that they are aware of everything going on in the service and have access to all relevant files. Once they leave the organisation, they will cease to have any access to client files or oversight of incidents and thus should not be held liable.

Second, the CQC will want to check if there are any blemishes on the proposed Registered Manager's records or major incidents reported under their watch, and also check how they ran previous services. If the person has held multiple posts as a Registered Manager and each of these organisations has had a CQC rating of 'requires improvement' this will arouse concern. Likewise, where all the services they have worked for are rated as 'good' or 'outstanding', this is a good indication that the person has a strong understanding of what their role entails. This check is also useful for an employer recruiting a Registered Manager to check how they have run services in the past before they take them on.

The critical question in this section asks whether they have ever been refused registration or disqualified from practising. This again seeks to establish any incidents that have occurred in a service they have managed which might have led to them being disqualified and/or any activities they were responsible for that led them to be discharged, for example a criminal record.

Health questions

The Registered Manager will be responsible for vulnerable people, so it is imperative that they are in good health.

Where they are not, it is important to declare this now to ensure both that the lives of the people they will be supporting are not put at risk and ensure that if any support is needed, employers know what to offer. The CQC will confirm whatever information is provided here with the Registered Manager's GP, so it is important to be truthful and forthcoming.

References

Like all job applications, the Registered Manager will need to submit references. Typically, they will ask for either one or two employers' references and a character reference. It is important to let referees know that they have been given as a reference because the CQC will not inform you of when they carry out their checks, so the referees will need advance notice.

Supporting documentation

Here you should include evidence to support all the information you have provided, such as:

- Proof of ID (passport or driving licence)
- DBS check
- CV
- Qualifications

Supporting notes

This section is not compulsory; however, I would suggest using it to write a personal statement detailing why the Registered Manager thinks they will be effective and responsible. In this statement, ensure qualifications and various experiences are linked to the five KLOEs mentioned in the provider application, illustrating either how the Registered Manager would perform their duties or has been doing so already.

Task

- Collate the information and documentation needed to complete the Registered Manager's application

- If you are to be the Registered Manager, write a personal statement to support your application

CHAPTER 7

Statement Of Purpose

In this chapter we will be looking in more detail at the Statement of Purpose (SoP). This is required by the CQC for registration purposes but is also a useful document for marketing and providing to potential clients.

This chapter will enable you to:

- Understand what the Statement of Purpose is, why you need one and its importance in the CQC application process

- Identify what information should be included in the SoP

- Create a comprehensive Statement of Purpose that is tailored to your care business

What is a Statement of Purpose?

The SoP is a written statement of what you do (your service provision), where you do it and who you do it for. In this way, it should be regarded as a general overview of your organisation. The SoP has dual importance; it is a requirement for CQC registration and also forms part of your marketing, helping you to acquire new clients. It is an opportunity to showcase what your organisation specialises in, how it delivers its service and the team driving it. As such, it should be as detailed as possible.

The CQC require that certain things be included in your SoP. Omission of any of these elements could lead to a delay in your application being processed, or even an outright rejection of your application. You want to avoid a rejection at all costs, as it typically means you will have to complete the whole registration process again. The CQC have a helpful SoP template and guidelines on their website[13] that I would highly recommend you follow. Even with this template, I think it's important to have a good understanding of what the document is about and its purpose so that you are well prepared for the interview.

What should you include?

Beyond the elements required by the CQC, there are no hard and fast rules as to what you should include in your

---

13   'Statement of Purpose'. Available at: www.cqc.org.uk/guidance-providers/registration-notifications/statement-purpose

SoP, but I recommend, at the very least, the following:

- The mission/vision of the organisation

- The type of service you provide and the location(s)

- The client group you cater for, eg children, the elderly, clients with dementia, adults with learning disabilities, etc

- What regulated activity you intend to provide

- The name of the Registered Manager along with their qualifications/skills/experience

- Names of those in senior management roles and teams for individual supported living services

- Any community organisations or activities your company is involved with

- The type of training you provide your staff or the mix of skills held by staff within the organisation

- A list of any other branches you may have

- Details of your headquarters

Let's look at each of these in more detail.

Mission/vision of your organisation

This sets the tone. It communicates who you are as an organisation and allows potential clients to understand your values as a company. In some cases, some historical background on how you got to where you are will help the CQC and potential clients to understand your journey, motivation and what you/the organisation represent.

The type of service you provide

This is where you set out what service you will provide and where. You may have multiple locations if you provide a supported living service, or have other services you are licensed to provide, such as one care home for elderly clients, a supported living service for adults with learning disabilities and a children's home. Each service must have its own SoP as each service will have its own staff, setting and unique requirements.

Your service users

Your SoP should clearly define who you are serving. As stated before, it is usually best to have a Statement of Purpose for each service/client group.

The regulated activities that you provide

Here, you should clearly delineate exactly what your service entails with regard to regulated activity – for example, you may provide only supported living or domiciliary care and be licensed to carry out regulated activities as part of this, or it may be that you only offer companionship and do not carry out any regulated activity as part of your service.

Registered Manager and senior staff

As mentioned in earlier chapters, the role of the Registered Manager in the organisation is an important one. Both clients' families and the authorities will want details on who is in charge of the service, not least because they need to know who to report to when there is a problem, but also to identify what experience and qualifications that person has so they can be assured that they are fit for the role. This is an opportunity to sell the skills, expertise and experience of the Registered Manager and why they are the ideal person to care for the service users.

The same applies for the senior management team as well as the Nominated Individual. All together, these are regarded as the key people of the organisation. In some cases, roles may be shared; for example, the role of Registered Manager may be shared by two people. Where this is the case, the profiles of both individuals must be detailed in the SoP.

Any community involvement

Although this is not a CQC requirement, it is a positive thing for your company and worth highlighting. It separates you from other organisations and, more importantly, connects you to the community. Being known in your community is like free marketing. It exposes opportunities within the community and also puts you in a unique position to help and give back. In addition, it means you are able to find out about activities and opportunities that may benefit your service users.

Staff training and skills

Just as they want to know about the level of expertise and experience the senior management team have, potential clients and their families will also want to know what skills your support staff have. The support and admin staff are the frontline workers within your organisation and are typically the first point of contact with service users or their families. Therefore, it is essential to not only highlight their experience and qualifications but also how you support ongoing professional development within the organisation and what training you make available. This will help to instil confidence that the staff in the organisation have the relevant training and qualifications necessary to support its clients.

Location and coverage

For those of you running a domiciliary care agency, you may only have the one branch, which will also be your head office. However, for those running supported living services and/or care homes, you may have multiple branches of the same service (for example, two or three supported living homes supporting adults with learning disabilities). Although each location should have its own SoP, it is helpful to mention your other branches in each document as it also acts as marketing material.

Headquarters

This is your main office or headquarters, where your admin team operate from. Generally, this will be your registered office that you would have listed with the CQC upon registration. The CQC will allocate a provider number to this address and it is where any important notices from the CQC or the local authority will be served. If your business is a limited company, the headquarters address that you notify the CQC of doesn't have to be the same address you registered with Companies House, but it must be where you run your business from – it could even be an office from your own home.

Contact information

This is simply information on how you can be contacted, and should include the usual contact details:

- Company address

- Telephone number(s) (including out of hours numbers)

- Email address

TASK

- Draft your Statement of Purpose and think about how you could repurpose some of the content as part of your marketing

CHAPTER 8

The CQC Interview

This chapter is about the CQC interview process and how to prepare for it. Both the Registered Manager and the Nominated Individual will be interviewed; typically these interviews happen on the same day, but they can sometimes be on two different days. In this chapter, I will discuss specifics about the interview process, the questions that you are likely to be asked, the information that you should prepare in advance to be able to fully answer these questions and the documents that you will need to take with you.

By the end of this chapter, you will understand:

- The CQC interview process

- How to identify the criteria you must meet to pass the CQC interview

- What policies and procedures you may be asked for/about at the interview

- The types of questions asked and information you'll need to prepare

- How to maximise your chances of success

- The common mistakes people make that lead to a rejection

On the day

What to expect

The interview is likely to take place via a Skype call rather than with an inspector visiting your premises – however, if the office is based at a home, they may visit to ensure it is suitable for staff and clients needing a private space to have a conversation. They might also want to examine how files are kept to ensure they are secure.

Length of interview

This will depend on the interviewer and how satisfied they are with your answers. In my experience, the interview was approximately one and a half to two hours, but I know of some who have had interviews lasting up to five hours with a follow-up call too. This is common where the same individual is the Nominated Individual and Registered Manager.

The interview criteria

The interviewer will be assessing your competency to run a care organisation. To do this, they will evaluate:

- The understanding of the relevant regulations.

- Level of experience – they will often ask for examples of real-life situations, expecting you to draw on previous experience and knowledge to provide full answers.

- Systems and processes – what is in place or intended to be in place to ensure the service operates efficiently.

- Your role in the business – what do you think is expected of you? What do you understand your role to be?

- Feedback mechanisms – how feedback will be collected and lessons learned.

- Communication – how information will be distributed to staff, service users and their families.

- Vulnerable clients – how do you assess clients who are vulnerable? For example, they might ask about the completion of BAME assessments.

- How the organisation handles complaints and incidents in terms of client care, responsiveness and follow-up actions.

- How the organisation audits itself to ensure it is meeting both its statutory obligations and its own targets and goals.

Policies

During the registration application you will have been asked to submit a number of policies. These will have been examined by the inspector and they will quiz you on them, so ensure you study them and have a good understanding of their content and how they relate to your business. If you can, have some pre-prepared examples of either how you intend to apply a policy in the organisation or how you have done so in a previous role.

There are certain policies that always seem to come up in CQC interviews, so it would be wise to ensure these are tailored to your company and not generic. There is no set order in which they ask you questions, so be prepared to answer questions about any or all of these at any time. Below is a list of policies frequently requested and scrutinised in the interview :

- Infection control – particularly crucial since the coronavirus pandemic

- Risk assessments – how you assess risk and what types of assessments you carry out

- Abuse – how this is handled within your organisation (both toward staff and service users)

- Complaints and feedback

- Whistle blowing

- Lone working

- Mental Capacity Act/Deprivation of Liberty Safeguards (soon to be changed to Liberty Protection Safeguards [LPS]) principles – how and when these can be used

- End of life care

- Respect, diversity, equality and consent

- Data protection and GDPR (General Data Protection Registration)

- Health and safety

There are other, more employee-specific policies that they may request, as well as company handbooks. For those offering supported living they may also ask to see tenancy agreements in particular and, if working with adults with learning disabilities, they will ask for easy-read versions. It is important that there are easy-read versions of any documentation that is to be shared with employees, service users or their families to show that you are an inclusive organisation.

Interview tips

Below are some top tips to help you in the CQC interview:

- Study all the policies requested by the inspector before the interview.

- Read and understand the regulations that govern the care industry and those that are specific to the area of care that you will be providing. The main ones that tend to come up are the Mental Capacity Act, Deprivation of Liberty Safeguards, and the fit and proper persons test. Identify the various governing bodies (RIDDOR/CQC) that are relevant to your organisation.

- Give full answers to all questions – the more detail the better. If your answers are sufficiently full you may find that you will have answered potential follow-up questions before they need to be asked. This demonstrates confidence and competency, and can reduce the length of the interview.

- When answering questions, where possible try to use real-life examples either based on your experience or an actual practical example to illustrate your point. Ensure the scenario or example is relevant to the question asked.

- Review sample questions and try some mock interview practice, taking into account the interview guidance notes and advice available on the CQC website.

And one useful tip: link questions together. For example, if you are asked about the Mental Capacity Act, provide an example but also link this question to the Deprivation of Liberty, as these two topics are often interlinked and questions on each usually follow on from each other.

By linking them even before you are asked, you will demonstrate your knowledge of the law and how it should be applied in practice. Another example would be linking how you handle complaints with how you deal with any safeguarding issues when they arise, along with implementing lessons learned and follow-up actions. These are almost always linked in practice and are a large part of providing care to vulnerable people.

Remember that the interview is your opportunity to present who you are, describe what you do, explain why you do it and highlight the skills, qualities and experience that you bring to your business that enables you to serve your client group efficiently and successfully. You should focus on quality of service provision, client care and maintaining the highest possible standards across all areas of work, but also show your passion for the industry, share your commitment, and bring your vision, mission and business story to life.

Don't panic. The inspector is human just like you – they are not there to trip you up. In fact, they want you to succeed, as there is the need for more good quality care services. They just need to ensure you have the right qualifications and experience.

Common mistakes and how to avoid them

There are some typical mistakes that are made during the interview stage of the application process, which can lead to a licence being denied. In this section, we'll cover some of the most common interview mistakes made.

The first is failure to understand the regulations governing the care industry. In any professional industry, understanding regulations and the relevant articles of law is essential. In the care sector it is even more important because you are responsible for some of the most vulnerable members of society.

Similarly, failure to properly demonstrate your experience and/or knowledge will damage your application. This is what confirms that you understand the responsibilities that come with owning and running a care business and so are an appropriate person to do so. In your role as Nominated Individual and/or Registered Manager, others' lives are in your hands. You must understand the nature and seriousness of your role to ensure you can deliver the best care in the safest possible manner.

Any apparent lack of understanding of the financial side of running a care business will raise a red flag with the interviewer. This is more relevant to the Nominated Individual, but anyone in a senior role should have a grasp of the business and what makes it financially viable. Lack of funds or mismanaged cash flow is one of the main reasons care services close – for the Nominated Individual in particular, they need to demonstrate that they have thought about how the service will be funded for at least the first twelve to twenty-four months, and until paying clients have been found and income is being generated.

A lack of understanding of company policies and the procedures that must be followed in a care business suggests to the interviewer that you don't have the necessary systems and processes in place to run your organisation safely, effectively and to the required standards. This will raise serious concerns for the CQC and is one of the most common reasons for an application to be rejected.

Remember, preparation is essential. The better prepared you are for your interview and the application process overall, the greater your chances of success.

Task

- Get a selection of CQC interview questions and ask someone to hold a mock interview with you

- Create flashcards with summaries of your company policies and test yourself on your knowledge of these

- Do the same for the most pertinent care sector regulations

CHAPTER 9

Marketing And Acquiring Clients

In this chapter, we will look at what action you must take to get your care business off the ground once your licence is approved. Marketing is fundamental to business success, as it is how you attract and retain clients. There are various techniques and strategies that you can implement to generate awareness of your business and secure clients.

By the end of this chapter, you will:

- Understand the importance of marketing your business and how this fits in with your wider business objectives

- Be able to identify some of the sources of clients in the care sector and how to approach them

- Understand how tenders work and how you can use them to find clients

- Feel confident in how to approach mental health teams and hospitals

- Know some techniques and strategies for reaching out to GP surgeries to source clients

The importance of marketing

Marketing is important for any business, regardless of the industry. It is just as important as cashflow. Its purpose is to create awareness about your service in order to attract paying customers, who form the lifeline of your business and drive your cashflow. Although in the care industry you may not necessarily consider or refer to the people using your service as 'customers', they are still paying clients, whether the bill is being met by them or through government funding.

There is some debate as to when the best time to start marketing is. Some would say after you obtain your licence, others say while you wait for your licence or maybe after the application has been submitted. From my experience, I would say the answer is as soon as possible, ideally once you have submitted your CQC application. There are a few good reasons to start so early.

Firstly, you need to create awareness about the service you are bringing to the local community, in particular your local authority, so that they know it exists. While the local authority will not start referring clients immediately, and certainly not before you have your licence, they may begin a dialogue with you about their needs and any service gaps they hope you could fill. The biggest challenge to many new care agencies is getting their service in front of the right commissioning team or brokerage. The commissioner/brokerage team are often overworked and have limited resources so don't have the luxury of time to go searching for new service providers. They are also often bombarded by providers daily and won't have time to check each one. If your service is meeting a specific need that they have, and this is clearly communicated in your initial outreach, there is a good chance that they will begin a dialogue with you.

Secondly, marketing early on could also help you find private clients. As mentioned previously, not all care provision requires a licence and CQC registration. People are in need of various types of support and care for all manner of reasons. For some potential clients, if no personal care is needed, you can offer your service even while you wait for your licence. For example, an elderly client may simply require companionship or assistance with tasks such as shopping, transportation, attending various activities in the community and so on. If you can attract and serve these types of clients you can start generating revenue and awareness of your business even before your licence is issued.

Types of marketing

There are various types of marketing strategy and techniques, and those you decide to use will depend on your clients. For example, marketing materials for private clients will be different to what you send to a local authority. It's important that you pick a strategy that reaches your target audience. For example, if you are targeting the local authority, I wouldn't suggest using social media, such as Instagram or Facebook advertisements; however, this may be an effective way to reach private individuals.

No marketing strategy is perfect and you may need to utilise trial and error, testing different techniques and tracking the results to see which gives the best outcomes. Some marketing techniques options are:

- Door-to-door leafleting

- Website and social media marketing – eg Facebook, Instagram, Twitter

- Directories, such as Bark, Care Sourcer and UKHSC

- Mainstream media – press releases or editorials, adverts to GPs

- Tendering websites such as Proactis

- Directly approaching local authority commissioners/social workers

- Directly approaching and/or advertising in hospitals, particularly discharge teams

The local authority

Every county has a local authority that provides care and support services for people in their area of control, from mental health support through to care in the community, support for those with learning difficulties and elderly care services.

The local authority is therefore a huge and important source of potential clients and one of your first marketing tasks should be to identify and approach your local authority. The people within the local authority who are responsible for approving care providers for use would be the commissioning or brokerage team. Social workers also play a major role in allocating providers to those requiring care. In my experience, the best ways to approach your local authority are:

- Targeted emails

- Follow-up phone calls

- Networking events

- Marketing materials such as brochures (particularly if you are offering specialist services or a supported living home)

When approaching them, try to find out what their pain point is – in other words, what they are short of – and focus your pitch on this. For example, in my experience, there was a shortage of wheelchair-accessible bungalows in the area and this was something my business could provide, so I made sure to highlight this to the local authority. Explain how your business can help them overcome their issues. If you have done your market research, this will have been a factor you took into account when deciding on what services you would be providing and creating your business plan.

Tenders

When seeking large or ongoing contracts, particularly in the public sector, 'tenders' are a term you'll encounter often. A tender is an invitation or request to pitch sent to multiple potential suppliers of a service required. These providers then respond with information about their service and costs, and submit a bid for the work. The buyer evaluates the responses and selects their preferred supplier. This is a common and popular way for local authorities and large companies to source care agencies that they then enter into a long-term contract with, often for a few years. For care companies, these contracts are an excellent source of income as they typically mean a constant flow of referrals.

In addition to the steady stream of clients, other benefits of tendering for work include guaranteed pay upon winning a contract. Unlike private clients, public organisations are bound by their contractual agreements to pay the awarded supplier. As such, winning a long-term contract or framework agreement can have a significant impact on the sustainability of your business.

In order to grow and evolve as a company and win larger contracts, you must present relevant case studies and demonstrable experience. Tendering for contracts as part of framework agreements or Dynamic Purchasing Systems (DPS) is an effective way of building this experience.[14] It also helps you to make contacts. Building relationships will enable you to connect and work with more buyers and gain valuable experience. Attend as many network events as you can to start building those relationships.

The tendering process

Tenders are usually published on websites such as Proactis, where you can sign up to be alerted when tenders are released.[15] Each company or local authority will have a tender document for you to complete that outlines their specific requirements. Some tenders can be quite short, others can be extremely lengthy with follow-up actions. This is dependent on the local authority and size and/ or length of the contract – some can be worth several thousands. What is important is to ensure you read and

---

14   For more information on framework agreements,
visit www.tenderconsultants.co.uk/framework-agreements
15   https://procontract.due-north.com/Register

complete all elements of the tender document and submit it within the deadline – very rarely will local authorities make exceptions to this.

Is tendering for you?

Tendering does sound like the perfect solution for all new care agencies; however, there are a few key things to consider. Firstly, can you fulfil the contract if you win? In other words, do you have the resources to deliver what is required? For example, do you have sufficient staff and/or capacity? This is primarily a concern for smaller companies where one individual is the Registered Manager, the carer, the administrator and more. Where you are also pitching a supported living service, the client will need to know that you have sufficient suitable properties available to meet their caseload.

Secondly, have you checked the financial thresholds? Do you meet the requirements? Often, suppliers will be asked for their minimum financial threshold, whether or not this exact phrasing is used. Generally, as a rule of thumb, it is advisable not to bid for projects with a budget that is greater than half of your annual turnover, so if the buyer states that the contract budget is £150k, your business should be turning over more than £300k for you to consider submitting a bid. It is also worth noting that in the public sector it is common for buyers to ask to see three years of accounts. The accounts will likely need to display the company name that you are currently trading under. If you are a new agency, this can pose a problem; however, some buyers will specify that new agencies can apply and will ask for different types of evidence in these cases.

Another factor to consider is whether you have the relevant experience – and you can back this up with evidence. In some tenders, the buyers will ask to see at least three relevant case studies as part of your bid. It is crucial that you have a variety of case studies written up, branded and ready to go. This will not only save time during the process, but will also allow you to assess whether a contract is the right fit for you.

You must also be sure you understand the payment terms – something many companies miss. Some contracts will only pay invoices after 30, 60 or even 90 days. You will in most cases need to pay your staff and suppliers much sooner than this. If it's a large contract, this means you could incur significant costs before receiving any income and must ensure you have the funds to cover this until your invoices are paid.

Finally, evaluate whether the contract will be profitable. It is understandable to feel enthusiastic when you see a contract for which you are eligible. However, before laying the groundwork for your bid, calculate your likely profit. While the contract budget might sound appealing, you need to assess what it will cost you to deliver the service and the resources the contract will require before moving forward. For example, are you expected to transfer staff across under Transfer of Undertakings (Protection of Employment Regulations)/TUPE? What is the expected pay? How often is work referred? These are all factors that could seriously impact your bottom line.

If you decide that tenders are definitely the approach for you, your first step is to register with as many sites as you can find to receive notifications of upcoming tenders in the areas you are interested in. A few good tender sites to get you started are:

- www.healthcare-tenders.co.uk

- www.proactis.com/uk

- www.gov.uk/contracts-finder

- www.londontenders.org

- www.supply2govtenders.co.uk

Once you have found one of interest to you, you can start bidding. Based on past experience, I would recommend following this tried-and-tested process:

- Attending any tender information sessions (most of these are online – it's a chance to meet some of the brokerage team/commissioners and ask questions about what is expected).

- Understand the payment terms and financial parameters and ensure you have sufficient funds to cover your costs until your invoices are paid. It is worth letting your bank know when you win a major bid as they may be able to give you an inexpensive funding option. You may also want to consider invoice factoring – where a company will pay the invoice to you for a fee and will then chase your invoice for you.

- Start to develop your tender response strategy. Most tenders are completed online but you can often save a draft for several weeks before the deadline, giving you plenty of time for rewrites and additions.

- Review recently awarded contracts – this is always good as a point of comparison as it helps you identify what information to include in your bid.

- Write a compelling bid. If you don't feel confident to do this yourself, find an excellent bid writer.

- Find and notify referees so that they can back up any evidence you provide.

- Check and triple check your bid and then submit your bid – and make sure it is on time!

Approaching healthcare providers

Another big source of clients is hospitals, mental health units and GPs. When you approach local hospitals and mental health units, speak to the discharge team; they will often be looking for suitable placements for those ready to be discharged into the community. Quite a number of people end up staying in hospital longer than they should because they have nowhere to go or can't find a suitable care agency.

The best person to discuss your service with is called a discharge coordinator – it is worthwhile getting friendly with this person, as they can be incredibly helpful and have day-to-day access to a steady stream of individuals requiring care. Many patients waiting to be discharged need care at home or in a supported living environment; by remaining in close contact with the discharge coordinator, you can offer proposals and position yourself as a go-to care provider – personal choice is a huge factor when commissioners assign care. It can also give you the opportunity to meet family members of those soon to be discharged and looking for carers for an urgent placement.

As well as hospitals, don't forget about GPs, they have a wealth of information and are a major part of the community. To approach local GPs, reach out to GP managers. They have knowledge of all their patients and will know a lot of potential service users within their community – they are often looking for agencies to make referrals to.

If there is a specialist in the GP surgery, such as a learning disability nurse or a mental health nurse, reach out to them – they will likely appreciate the resources. They are also part of a network of community professionals, such as mental health teams, complex care teams and multidisciplinary teams. If you build a good relationship with these people, they have the power to invite you to upcoming team meetings where you can discuss your service with their team.

Of course, printed brochures can also be hand delivered to GP surgeries and should be addressed to the manager. If you get friendly with reception staff, they may display these for you in the waiting room.

Task

- Sign up to receive notifications from relevant tender sites

- Compile a list of contacts you could approach to offer your services

- Write and design a marketing brochure and distribute it to local GP surgeries and hospital discharge units

CHAPTER 10

Client Care

This chapter discusses the importance of creating and implementing a client care charter, committing to quality standards and ensuring that your business is fully compliant with all regulations. Your client acquisition and onboarding process should be seamless and a thorough assessment needs to be conducted for all new clients to properly evaluate their care needs. You will also need to draft a proposal of how you intend to provide care for each individual client, which should be as person-centred as possible

By the end of this chapter, you should be able to:

- Confidently navigate the process of acquiring new clients

- Undertake a thorough needs assessment to ensure client care is tailored to the individual

- Know the importance of preparing a thorough client proposal for each new client

- Explain how property adjustments work and how they are carried out

- Describe the client onboarding process

- Know how to conduct a new client assessment

- Understand the importance of developing a care plan for each client

- Understand the best way to make the transition to the new environment as seamless as possible for a new client

In order to effectively deliver quality client care, other tasks that you will need to complete and/or manage are:

- Staff rotas

- Staff training where necessary

- Menu plans if meals are supplied

- Planning property adjustments – handrails, ramps, seats in showers and bed rails

Client acquisition

Even if you have not yet had your interview or got your licence, as part of your CQC application process you should have put in place the systems and processes that your business will operate by. This should include the client journey, the first step of which is the client acquisition process.

The acquisition process itself consists of several components:

- The initial client assessment

- Proposal

- Formulating and reviewing care plans and transition plans

- Drafting a service user guide

- Briefing staff

- Issuing marketing materials and welcome packs to clients, families and professionals

Client assessment

The client assessment is a crucial step in the process and it is important that you understand what purpose this serves. The assessment is the first step in identifying the specific needs that the person you will be supporting has. It gives you a chance to get to know them as an individual, which is beneficial both for you and the potential client. In some cases, you may be talking to a family member who is representing the individual, or to social services. You should speak to all concerned in the person's current care to acquire a full picture of their needs – for example, you might need to speak to the person's psychiatrist, district nurse and previous care providers.

The assessment helps to determine if you are the right service for the person. For example, if you specialise in learning disability only, a dementia client would not be the best fit for you. You also need to identify if the person needs special equipment and, if they do, whether they will provide it or if you have to ensure it is in place.

Understanding a potential client's needs enables you to work out what kind and level of staffing is required: how many carers will be required for what activities and over what length of time. This also highlights what training needs there may be.

Overall, the assessment helps you to gain a broad understanding of the individual and whether you can provide them with quality care, and give you an idea of what strategies you may need to put in place in the proposal.

Proposal

The purpose of the proposal is to outline how you intend to provide the care and support your clients need and to identify areas where you can help to improve their lives. Some agencies provide a skeleton proposal; I recommend being as detailed as possible, ensuring you are highlighting the needs or challenges identified from your initial assessment and then what solutions you can provide to those issues. As well as offering solutions to problems potential clients are facing, you should also include ways of enhancing their lives. Local authorities are focused on outcomes so, where possible, you want to show how your care is improving your clients' lives.

Your proposal should:

- Be as in-depth as possible, to make it easier for the service user or local authority to understand your service and what you can offer.

- Include costings – the proposal should include an accurate estimation of how much it will cost you to care for the individual. It's important you get this right to ensure you are earning enough to pay staff and sustain your business.

- Set out the staffing details – who will be providing the required care, what relevant experience and training they have and any specialist training they will require. For example, a person with challenging behaviour might require that two staff members are with them at any one time.

- Identify the challenges for the service user and explain how you will assist with these. Explain how you intend to involve the service user and support them to be as independent as possible within the community.

- If you're proposing a supported living or domiciliary care service, detail any adjustments you may need to make to the property to ensure care and support can be delivered safely.

Care plans and transition plans

Once your proposal has been accepted by the family or the local authority you will need to create a more in-depth care plan detailing how you intend to provide the necessary care on a daily basis.

It is also important to prepare a transition plan. This details how the person concerned will start to receive care from you. Having a plan that all parties agree on ensures there will be a smooth transition to your service. For example, if the person is being discharged from a mental health hospital to your supported home, you may want to start with an introduction to the staff for the service user and their family, to talk about expectations and how the individual will be supported. The transition plan might include some visits to the new site in the days leading up to the move; if so, the dates and durations of these visits should be included in the plan. The plan should also include a review date, to ensure the service user has settled in with the service and whether adjustments need to be made.

There are various strategies that you can implement to ensure that clients are made to feel welcome and that their transition to your facility is a seamless one. A few we have used in our supported living service are to:

- Provide clients with a service user guide. This gives the service user and their family information on how your service works, along with contact details and the location of the office and a process for providing feedback or making a complaint.

- For supported living services, ensure the tenancy agreement is understood and signed. Always have an easy-read version so that it is accessible to everyone.

- Offer opportunities to visit and meet potential staff at your office or at the supported living service.

All care packages should be reviewed regularly to ensure you are continuing to meet the needs and expectations of your service users. Local authorities will expect reviews to be carried out regularly. Particular attention should be paid in the first six weeks so that issues can be identified and client care plans adjusted accordingly.

Staff recruitment and selection

Once you have a good understanding of your new client's needs, you need to ensure you have staff that are qualified and experienced to support that individual. In some cases, you may need to provide training to staff already in your organisation to give them the necessary skills, in other cases you may need to recruit new specialist staff.

More and more, local authorities and families want to be involved in shaping their care packages. It is important, where you can, to involve service users in the staff selection process and consider any preferences they might have. In the eyes of the CQC, this is regarded as offering 'person-centred care', a necessity for lots of families but also something the CQC will grade your organisation on.

Task

- Write a skeleton proposal that you can expand on and add detail to following client assessment

- Create a care plan for a fictitious client

- Create a transition plan for a fictitious client

- Draft your service user guide

CHAPTER 11

Compliance, Feedback And Review

In this chapter we will look at compliance monitoring and review, and why this is important in the care sector. Once your care business is established, you must be able to demonstrate that your organisation is not only compliant with regulations, but that you are regularly monitoring operations to ensure things remain that way. This is important not least because the CQC will want to see evidence of how you are monitoring compliance. It also ensures you continue to operate safely

By the end of this chapter, you should understand:

- What is involved in compliance, monitoring and review

- The importance of spot checks

- The benefit of mock inspections

How to monitor your organisation

Within the care sector, you must demonstrate ongoing compliance. This entails monitoring how your organisation is running, ensuring staff are doing what they are supposed to be doing, when and where they are supposed to be doing it. By continually monitoring your organisation you will be able to get regular feedback to ensure your clients are receiving the service you promised them.

Below are some examples of the types of checks you should be regularly carrying out on your organisation:

- Spot checks led by senior staff

- Reviewing care notes and handover notes

- Following up on incidents and implementing any new learning as soon as practicable

- Providing opportunities for staff, service users, professionals and families to provide feedback such as anonymous complaints, compliments and suggestion boxes in the office, questionnaires, focus group sessions and online feedback

- Weekly meetings with senior management team

- Regular meetings with frontline staff

- Medication audits

Spot checks

Spot checks are essentially unannounced visits by yourself or a senior member of the team to either a registered home that you run or to a client's home. These inspections give you a chance to see your support workers in action and ensure that they are carrying out their duties as they should, and may include other checks, such as a medication audit. The inspection is also an opportunity to speak to the client and get feedback on the service they are receiving – they may have suggestions for improvements that can be made. With spot checks, there is no time to tidy things up – you should take the opportunity to check daily logs if you are using a paper-based method. If these are kept online then you should be checking these frequently.

Feedback

Seeking feedback about your service should become a regular part of your daily business practices. It's important to ensure your service continues to meet the needs of those you serve and the best way of doing so is to ask them directly. Feedback should be requested from anyone involved in your service – current or previous clients, their families, other professionals you work with, and staff.

You can collect feedback in various ways and formats, including survey questionnaires, group discussions, suggestion boxes. Again, be sure to have an easy-read version for those who may need it, to ensure accessibility to all.

Feedback is only useful if it is actioned and used to improve your service, so you also want to have systems in place to follow up and act on the feedback you receive. Keep track of this so that you have evidence to show how feedback has been incorporated into your organisation and the improvements this has led to.

Regular team meetings

Regular meetings with your team allow you to keep up to date with what is happening in your organisation. As your business grows, you may no longer be 'on the ground' day to day, so you will have to depend on your staff to ensure processes are being followed.

Regular meetings will keep you informed of any issues, actions that have been taken and next steps to be implemented. Where there have been incidents such as complaints or safeguarding issues, the meetings are a place to discuss how these are being handled and what lessons have been learned.

Meetings give your staff an opportunity to air any challenges they may be facing or concerns they have, in a safe environment. It is also an opportunity for you to share any updates taking place within the organisation and ensure that information is being disseminated down to everyone within your organisation, not just the senior management with whom you may be in contact more regularly.

Audits

Internal auditing allows you to identify and monitor trends within your organisation. This highlights areas where your business is struggling or performing well, and if it is missing or achieving set targets. For example, you might have a target of less than five complaints per month and two incidents reported to the CQC, yet monitoring your data reveals that for a six-month period you have had at least ten complaints and five incidents each month. Monthly audits mean you are forced to confront these numbers and examine the root cause to find a solution and meet your target. This kind of reporting is something CQC will also look at, to see if you are paying attention to emerging or continuing trends and making necessary changes.

Areas they are likely to look at would be:

- Complaints or incidents – how many have occurred over a set period and what was the outcome?

- Safeguarding reports – how many have occurred over a set period and what were the resolutions and outcomes?

- Staff turnover and retention figures

- Mock inspection results

Mock inspections

A mock inspection is a simulated practice run of the official CQC inspection – which are likely to occur every year. You can carry out mock inspections yourself or use an external consultant. You should begin these mock inspections when your care business has been up and running for a little while – I recommend not leaving it too long after you get your first client. We carried out our first mock inspection a month after we were assigned three new clients and had at least two mock inspections within our first year.

Why are these important? CQC inspections can literally make or break an organisation, so it is imperative you are fully prepared. It's almost as if you are being re-interviewed to keep your licence. The more frequently you carry out a mock inspection, the more prepared you will be for the real thing. It also familiarises your staff with the process and, most importantly, ensures your paperwork (such as risk assessments) is always up to date so that you're not caught out by any last-minute inspections. Mock inspections will highlight areas where you can improve, so you can work your way towards obtaining an outstanding rating at that real inspection. This is particularly the case if you are using an external consultant for mock inspections, as you can benefit from a fresh set of eyes.

Task

- Draw up a schedule for regular meetings

- Decide how you will collect feedback and create a template for this (eg online survey questionnaire, comment cards, a suggestion box)

- Create a mock inspection template

Conclusion

We have reached the end of the book; by now you should be able to set up and structure a care business, prepare a comprehensive business plan and navigate the CQC registration process with ease. I also advised how to write your Statement of Purpose, fill out the CQC application form and supply the necessary documentation, and then succeed at the CQC interview. Looking past the application process, we covered how to market your business and source new clients, implement policies, procedures and ways of working to deliver the highest quality client care.

Armed with all of the above, you are now ready to launch your care business with confidence, having gained the necessary tools, knowledge and resources to achieve success in this rewarding sector.

Like any business, you will get out of it what you put into it. If you have the good and welfare of others at heart, you will be a place that hospitals, local authorities and other clients are happy to refer people to. I wish you every success for the future.

The Author

Kemi Madumere is a successful serial entrepreneur, author and speaker, with a master's degree in business. She is the co-director of Compass Supported Living, a successful care agency based in London, and also a co-director for Brighter Futures Foundation, a CIC offering day opportunities and experiences for adults with learning disabilities.

Having run a property business for several years as a director of a specialist housing provider, she moved into the care industry to provide supported living services. Her business acumen plus attention to comprehensive and efficient processes and systems have enabled her company to become one of the leading care agencies in the UK.

🌐 www.gettingintocare.co.uk

📷 www.instagram.com/gettingintocare